Plymouth Hoe

Plymouth Hoe
by
Derek Tait

Driftwood Coast Publishing

Frontispiece : A young girl sings on the Hoe during the wartime dances.

First published 2008

Driftwood Coast Publishing
PO Box 7,West Park,Plymouth,PL5 2YS.
© Derek Tait, 2008

The right of Derek Tait to be identified as the author
of this work has been asserted in accordance with the
Copyrights, Designs and Patents Act 1988.

Contents

Acknowledgements

Photo credits : The Driftwood Coast Photo Library, Derek Tait, Tina Cole, Steve Johnson and Chris Goddard.
I have tried to track down the copyright holders of all photos used and apologise to anyone who hasn't been mentioned.

Bibliography

Books:
Drake's Island Adventure Centre (Drake's Island Council 1970s).
Images of England : Plymouth by Derek Tait (Tempus 2003).
Mount Edgcumbe House and Country Park: A Guide by Cynthia Gaskell Brown (Mount Edgcumbe Country Park Jan 2003).
Plymouth at War by Derek Tait (Tempus 2006).
The Story of Plymouth Hoe by Marion Beckford (Plymouth Guild).

Websites:
Steve Johnson's Cyberheritage site at http://www.cyber-heritage.co.uk/
Robert Lenkiewicz at www.robertlenkiewicz.org/new-hoe-summer-theatre
Brian Moseley's Plymouth Data website at: www.plymouthdata.info

Newspapers
Evening Herald
Western Morning News

Driftwood Coast Publishing
© Derek Tait 2008

Introduction

The Hoe or 'Hoh', as it was once called, means the spur of a hill or a high place. The Hoe has been a popular gathering place for hundreds of years. It is steeped in history. From ancient times, limestone drawings of the giants, Gog and Magog were cut into the grass on the Hoe. They would have been there when Francis Drake played his much written about game of bowls as he got word of the Armada approaching.

During the time that Francis Drake was Mayor, a mariner's compass was newly erected on the Hoe on Wynderygge Hill. It survived until 1730.

The Hoe witnessed the Civil War in the 1640s and the building of the Citadel in the 1660s. A windmill once stood on the top of the Hoe and this is shown on a Civil War map of 1643. It was reported that its vane was shot off during an attack from the fort at Mount Batten. Another landmark on the Hoe was the Trinity Obelisk which was destroyed in 1882. The triangular Obelisk served as a navigation marker for ships in the Sound. Workmen removed the obelisk under the direction of a Mr John Pethick, a local contractor. Crowds gathered around to see the obelisk blown apart by gunpowder on 18th October, 1882. The reason that the obelisk was destroyed was because two days later on 20th October, 1882, the foundation stone for Smeaton's Tower was laid in its place.

For many years, the Hoe was just rough grass where sheep and cows grazed. In the 1880s, the Hoe took on its present layout when new paths, grassed areas and monuments were laid out. At the same time, the Hoe area was generally tidied up. Some of the present day buildings and monuments that were erected during the late 1800s include the Marine Biological Association's Aquarium, The Belvedere, Drake's Statue, the

National Armada Memorial, Norrington's Fountain and of course, Smeaton's Tower. Other attractions during the Victorian period included the Camera Obscura, the Bandstand and the Promenade Pier.

The Hoe has, for hundreds of years, attracted many thousands of people who have gathered for various events. In 1625, ten thousand troops paraded here during a visit by King Charles I and his Queen. Executions also drew large crowds especially when three young marines met death by firing squad in 1797.

In 1815, people gathered on the Hoe to see the captured Napoleon on the deck of the ship, Bellerphon. When the Prince of Wales married in 1863, five thousand children sang in unison on the Hoe. In 1967, thousands of people waited on the Hoe for the return of Sir Francis Chichester after his single handed voyage. Of course, there have been many, many more events over the years which have also attracted very large crowds.

Between the wars, the Tinside Lido was built together with the limestone fronted bathing houses, the terraces and the changing rooms. The cliff paths towards the foreshore were built and electric lighting was installed around the bathing area in 1932.

During the War years, the Hoe proved again to be a very popular meeting place as people danced on the promenade on warm evenings in defiance of the German bombing. During 1941, the bandstand and Promenade Pier were bombed and destroyed.

The Hoe has seen many changes over the years. Although it may seem like not a lot has changed in the last 30 years, this period has included the removal of the Hoe Theatre, the removal of the Hoe Floral Cafe, the removal of the Mallard Cafe overlooking the Sound (replaced by the Plymouth Dome), the long overdue refurbishment of the Lido, the erection of the RAF and Allied Forces Monument, the fire that destroyed the Grand Hotel and the restoration of Smeaton's Tower.

Today, wandering around Plymouth Hoe, it's easy to imagine past generations once visiting the buildings and monuments that still stand there today. Hopefully, this book will inform readers about the varied history of the Hoe and also prove interesting to anyone who is seeing the Hoe and all of its attractions for the first time.

One:
Gog and Magog

The giants as they may have appeared on the Hoe.

One of the earliest recorded mentions of the area comes from Geoffrey of Monmouth who wrote about Plymouth Hoe in 1136 when he told the story of the giant, Gogmamgog (which he originally calls Goemagot). The story of Gogmagog's Leap told how Brutus, the great-grandson of the Trojan hero, Aeneas, came to Albion with his followers and decided to settle. He called the land 'Britain' which was meant to be a derivation of 'Brutus'. Brutus drove out the giants who inhabited the land sending them into the mountains in the west. One day, while holding a festival at the port where they first landed, Brutus and his men were attacked by a group of giants who they killed all except one who was called Gogmagog. He was said to be 12 cubits high. A cubit would have been about one and a half feet which would have made Gogmagog about 18 feet tall. It was said that Gogmagog could wield an uprooted oak tree as a weapon. Brutus kept Gogmagog alive so that he could wrestle with Corineus, the then Duke of Cornwall, who loved to wrestle with giants. When the opponents met for the first time, Gogmagog gripped Corineus so tightly around his middle that he broke three of his ribs. This enraged Corineus who then threw

Gogmagog off nearby cliffs and he fell to his death on the jagged rocks below. This was all said to have happened on Plymouth Hoe and the chalk giants that once appeared on the Hoe represented this wrestling match.

There is a record of the chalk cut giant being on Plymouth Hoe in 1486 and a record in the City Archive shows a receipt for a bill for cleaning and weeding the giant. The bill was paid by the Earl of Edgcumbe. It is uncertain when the figure first appeared. Town records from 1486 onwards call the figure Gogmagog but in Carew's Survey of Cornwall in 1602, he refers to there being two figures on the slopes of the Hoe, both wielding clubs. One was bigger than the other and he calls them Gog and Magog, splitting the name into two halves. Several years later though, the smaller figure was being referred to as Corineus so the figures obviously commemorated the earlier wrestling match mentioned by Geoffrey of Monmouth . The figures were unfortunately destroyed when the Citadel was built in the reign of King Charles II.

The Royal Citadel now stands where the figures of Gog and Magog were once laid out.

Two:
Sir Francis Drake

Francis Drake was born at Crowndale near Tavistock in around 1540. Perhaps the most famous story connecting Drake with Plymouth Hoe is the one of how he played bowls on 19th July 1588 with his fellow captains. When news was brought to them that the Armada had been spotted off the Lizard, Drake announced that they still had time to finish the game and beat the Spaniards as well. Many people have dismissed the story as a myth and if the game did take place, it wasn't where the current bowling green is on the Hoe now. Interestingly, the game was banned by law at the time and the reason given was that it caused people to neglect their archery practice. It's possible that the rich had private games in their own gardens. Drake had a house with a garden in Looe Street and John Hawkins had a residence closer to the harbour. If the game did take place on the Hoe, it's likely to have been in the area of the much quarried Lambhay Hill where the Citadel now stands which would have also been near the giants, Gog and Magog. From here, Drake would have had an excellent vantage point of the Sound right across to Rame. In the only remaining copy of Phoenix Britannicus, published in 1624, only 36 years after the event, the story is told as fact and states that the match did indeed take place on the Hoe.

An old painting of Drake and his men playing bowls on the Hoe.

Three:
The Citadel

King Charles II realised the importance of Plymouth as a port during the
Dutch Wars between 1664 and 1667 and a decision was made to build
the Royal Citadel. It incorporated a smaller fort which had stood there

during the times of Francis Drake.

Building work began in 1665 under the watch of Sir Bernard De Gomme, the Chief Engineer. A small harbour was included where ships could berth safely under the watch and safety of the guns of the Citadel. The harbour is now the Corinthian Yacht Club.

The foundation stone for the Citadel was laid by Lord Bath on 18th July 1666.

The gun emplacements not only point out to sea but also point into the town. This is because the town supported Parliament during the Civil War instead of Charles' father, Charles I.

The Citadel is built of local limestone and the ornate main gate on Hoe Road was designed by Sir Thomas Fitz. There is a gap below the tablet above the gate which was originally built to house a statue of Charles II. However, it now holds three cannonballs instead. The tablet reads, 'Carolus secundus dei gratia magnae brittaniae franciae et hiberniae rex' and features the date, 1670. The gate is built of Portland Stone. There was originally a drawbridge, over a moat, leading to the entrance, but this was removed in 1888 when the moat was filled in to make a garden area. Interestingly, the moat, although there for 200 years, never held water.

An old engraving showing the view from the Citadel towards the Sound. Drake's Island and Mount Edgcumbe can be seen in the background.

Four:
Drake's Island

Drake's Island, Plymouth

Francis Drake said, 'He who holds the island, holds the town'. The first recorded name for the island was 'St Michael's' in 1135 named after the chapel that was built upon it. Later on, it was renamed St Nicholas's Island. From the 16th Century, some people referred to it as Drake's Island but it appeared as St Nicholas's Island on maps until well into the 19th Century. It is only really in the last 100 years or so that the island has fully adopted the name Drake's Island.

The island was fortified in 1549 as a defence against the French and the Spanish. Barracks for 300 men were then built there in the late 1500s. Drake sailed from here in 1577 to circumnavigate the world. When he returned aboard the Golden Hind, early in the morning of Michaelmas in 1580, he called to a fisherman to ask if Queen Elizabeth was still alive. He knew that if she had died while he had been away, and Mary Queen of Scots was on the throne, that England would be no place for him.

Drake hid the Golden Hind on the southern shore of Drake's Island and waited while a messenger was sent to London to see if the Queen approved of his voyage. Once he knew he had Royal approval, Drake sailed into harbour with more treasure than any Englishman had ever seen.

In 1583, Drake became governor of the island. In the year of the Armada in 1588, Drake had the defences built up on the island. He felt that eight culverins built on the island would protect the Sound from any invading warship. Drake had six of his best cannons from his ship 'Revenge' landed on the island. He knew that any hostile ship, that wished to sail into the Cattewater, would have to sail within 660 yards of the island's batteries. The passage was made impregnable on the strength of experienced English gunners and their weapons.

Drake made sure that men and their guns remained on the island constantly. To keep the men awake, he stationed a night guard on the island and drafted in a selection of bankers, men of property, lawyers and chief merchants. He knew that they had the most to lose if they fell asleep and the enemy crept into harbour. With the thought of all their assets in Plymouth, they made sure that they stayed awake!

During the reign of Charles II, Drake's Island was described as the most evil prison in English history and became the permanent home for political prisoners. The Roundhead, Robert Lilburne died here after being imprisoned on the island in 1665. He had been given a life sentence for his role in the death of Charles I. Another Roundhead, General John Lambert was also imprisoned on the island after being moved from Guernsey. He was imprisoned from 1662 to his death, on the island, in the Winter of 1683.

Also imprisoned on the island at the time were clergy who were persecuted during the great Ejectment of 1662. These included Puritan and Cromwellian clergy who refused to stop preaching even though they were deprived of their living. One much loved Baptist pastor, Abram Cheare, who preached at the Old George Street Baptist Chapel, was locked away on the island from 1665 until he died in 1668.

Common ailments of prisoners on the island included dropsy, gaol fever and starvation. Few survived such harsh conditions.

During the two world wars, fortifications for defence were hastily built. The War Office held on to the island throughout the Second World War and after but announced in 1956 that it was no longer needed for defence purposes.

In 1960, there was an attempt to remove the concrete fortifications from the island but this left it in a state of devastation with a great deal of damage being caused. During 1961, young men of Plymouth were enlisted by the Old Plymouth Society and the island was cleared of debris and many of the buildings were repaired.

The War Office kept the island until 1963 when Plymouth City Council obtained a lease from the Crown so that they could turn it into a Youth Adventure Centre. The centre opened in 1964 which was also the year when the island first got a mains water supply.

The island got its first telephone line in May 1987 using a cable that followed the line of the water mains supply pipe. In March 1989,the Mayflower Trust gave up its lease and the island reverted back to the Crown.

The island still contains military buildings from the Napoleonic era as well as an MOD mast.

In 1995, Dan McCauley, the former Plymouth Argyle chairman, bought the island for £384,000 from the Crown Estate.

Interestingly, Drake's Island is the cap on a volcano that erupted millions of years ago. Deposits of the volcanic rock can be found on the shores between Kingsand and Fort Picklecombe.

An aerial view of Drake's Island showing the landing jetty and fortifications.

Five:
Smeaton's Tower

Smeaton's Tower was built by John Smeaton on the Eddystone Reef in 1759. There had been two previous lighthouses in the same location. The first was built by Henry Winstanley in 1695. Unfortunately, seven years later, during a storm, it was washed away taking its builder with it.
The second lighthouse was built in 1711 by John Rudyerd but it was destroyed by a fire in 1755. Work commenced on Smeaton's Tower in December 1756 to replace the damaged lighthouse. Smeaton's Tower would still be there today but the rock underneath it was undermined by the sea. James Douglass built a new lighthouse on an adjoining rock. It was felt that if Smeaton's Tower was left standing beside the new lighthouse, that it could eventually collapse onto the new lighthouse if the rock beneath it became even more undermined. It was decided to blow it up but a Mr FJ Webb suggested that it should be dismantled and erected on the Hoe where the Trinity House Navigational Obelisk once stood. This was quite a task and the lighthouse was removed stone by stone and rebuilt on the Hoe with a new base to support it. The original base can still be seen beside the present Eddystone Lighthouse.
On 24th September,1884,the Lord Mayor opened Smeaton's Tower on the Hoe to the public.

Smeaton's Tower in it's original position on Eddystone Reef.

Six:
Memorials

This photo features the Naval Memorial, the Drake Memorial and the Armada Memorial. After the First World War, it was decided to build a memorial to commemorate the men who had died in the war but who had no known graves. It was felt that the members of the army could be remembered on other memorials but individual memorials were built in Plymouth, Chatham and Portsmouth to remember Naval personnel. The memorials were built to a unique design which also served as a marker to shipping.

The memorials were designed by Sir Robert Stodart Lorimer who also designed the Scottish National War Memorial in Edinburgh and several war cemeteries in Germany. Each memorial in the three cities comprise of a central tower made of Portland Stone with four buttresses on each corner arch featuring a lion. On the sides of the original memorial are brass plaques bearing the names of 7,000 sailors who lost their lives in the First World War.

Sub Lieutenant HRH Prince George unveiled the memorial on 29th July,1924.

After the Second World War, the memorial was extended to commemorate the recent war dead and a sunken area was built on the inland side of the original memorial. The designer was Sir Edward Maufe who incorporated statues of Neptune and Amphitrite. There are also two sculptures of sailors featured as part of the memorial. These were designed by Charles Wheeler. Other statues include a Royal Marine and a member of the Maritime Regiment of the Royal Artillery. Both were designed by William McMillan.

The panels in the sunken garden area contain the names of a further 16,000 men. The new part of the memorial was opened by Princess Margaret on 20th May, 1954.

The copper globe on top of the memorial features a dent which is clearly visible. This is a remnant of German bombing during the Second World War.

Drake's statue on the Promenade of the Hoe.

The statue of Drake was unveiled by Lady Fuller Drake on 14th February, 1884. Lady Drake was the wife of Sir Francis Fuller Drake who was a descendant of Drake's brother, Thomas.

When it was first suggested that a statue of Drake be erected, there was little interest shown and there was difficulty raising the money to pay for it. Meanwhile, the Duke of Bedford had paid for a statue of Drake to be erected at Tavistock. The Duke allowed for a replica to be made of the original statue, at a lower cost, and it was this replica that was erected on the Hoe. At the unveiling ceremony, there were 6,000 people present together with several bands, guards of honour, various members of the forces and 2,000 children. A salute from 17 guns was fired to mark the occasion.

Between the Naval Memorial and the Hoe Lodge Gardens, there is a cross with the number '3' embedded in the pavement. This marks the spot where three Royal Marines were executed by firing squad on 6 July, 1797. Their names were Lee, Coffy and Branning and they were found guilty of attempting to excite a mutiny at Stonehouse Barracks. Another Marine, M Gennis was convicted of a similar crime and sentenced to 1000 lashes and transported to Botany Bay for life.

The incident was reported in the Sherborne and Yeovil Mercury on Monday 10th July,1797. It read:

'PLYMOUTH, July 8 - On Wednesday morning an express arrived here from the War-Office, with a warrant for the execution of Lee, Coffy, and Branning, three marines who were last week tried by a General Court-Martial, and found guilty of an attempt to excite a mutiny among the marine corps at Stone-house Barracks and on Thursday at 12 o'clock the troops at this place and in the neighbourhood, consisting of the Sussex fencible cavalry, four companies of the royal artillery, the Lancashire, East Devon and Essex regiments of militia, the 25th regiment of foot, royal independent invalids, and Plymouth volunteers, assembled on the Hoe, and formed in a half circle in order to witness the execution. M Gennis, another marine tried for a similar crime, and sentenced to receive 1000 lashes, and to be afterwards transported to Botany Bay for life, was brought on the ground soon after twelve o'clock, and received 500 lashes, and then conveyed back to Stone-house

Barracks. At half past one o'clock, Lee, Coffy and Branning were marched from the Citadel under the escort of a party of marines, with a coffin before each, preceded by the band of that corps playing the Dead March in Saul.
The former was attended by the Rev. Dr. Hawker; and the two latter by a Roman Catholic priest, who after praying with them near an hour, quitted them, and they all three knelt on their coffins for a few minutes, when an officer of marines came and drew the caps over their faces, and a party of twenty marines immediately came down and put a period to their existence by discharging the contents of their muskets through their bodies, after which all the regiments marched round them in solemn procession, the whole forming, perhaps, one of the most awful scenes that the human eye ever witnessed. They all behaved in a manner becoming their melancholy situation, and apparently very resigned and penitent. About thirty thousand people were supposed to be present at the execution'.

There was more to the execution than mentioned in the newspaper though. Ten thousand men of the Fleet and garrison were there to watch them die and most of Plymouth appeared to have turned out too. When the three men faced the firing quad and the shots were fired, Coffy and Branning fell forward, dead, into their coffins. However, Lee was not hit and had to go through the whole procedure again. The reserve firing squad lined up, took aim and fired but again Lee was untouched. Once more, they loaded up, took aim but again missed Lee. In the end, a sergeant came up behind him and shot him dead at close range. It seems odd that the firing squad missed Lee three times and perhaps there was some sympathy with him amongst the troops.
Earlier fourteen seamen had been hanged at the yardarm on their ships in the Sound.
This was to be Plymouth's last public execution.

This photo shows the South African War Memorial overlooking a pre-war view of the city. The memorial is 43 feet high and is made of red granite mounted on a green base. It contains four bronze panels. One is inscribed, 'Towards Another World'. It was designed by Emile Fuche MVO, and is dedicated to HRH Prince Christian Victor.

The three other panels are the work of Onslow Whiting and include one facing North which features the charge of the Devonshire Regiment at Waggon Hill. It is inscribed with the words:

'One point in our position was occupied by the enemy the whole day but at dusk in a very heavy rainstorm they were turned out of the position at the point of the bayonet in the most gallant manner by the Devon Regiment led by Colonel Park. General White's despatch 7 January 1900'.

Another panel bears the inscription:

'This obelisk is erected by Alfred Mosely to the memory of Christian Victor Prince of Schleswig-Holstein and to the officers, non-commissioned officers and men of the Gloucestershire, Somerset and Devonshire Regiments who fell during the Boer War, 1899-1902.
Onslow Whiting. November 1902'.

A further panel shows the Somerset and Gloucestershire Regiments in action.

A closer view of the South African War Memorial.

The Plymouth War Memorial is set back from the Promenade on the Hoe and is situated at the junction of Lockyer Street and Citadel Road. It serves as a memorial to the soldiers who died in the First World War. It was unveiled on 19th May 1923. The memorial was designed by HL Thornley, AV Rooke and J Leighton Fouracre. The statue, which stands over eight feet tall, was designed by Birnie Rhind.

The National Armada Memorial.

The foundation stone was laid for the National Armada Memorial, in the presence of Naval, Military and Civic representatives, by the Mayor of the Borough, Alderman H J Waring, Esquire, JP, on Thursday 19th July, 1888, which marked the three hundredth anniversary of the first sighting of the Spanish Armada while Drake played bowls on the Hoe.

The National Armada Memorial was designed by Herbert Gribble and the pedestal was made using granite from quarries at Gunnislake. A bronze statue of Britannia, measuring 11 feet and six inches, stands on the pedestal. The sculptor was Charles May.

On the north side of the monument is the inscription, 'England expects that every man will do his duty'. There is also a bust of Sir Francis Drake, the arms of Queen Victoria and a tablet showing the war vessels of the Victorian period.

Also commemorated on the other sides of the memorial are Lord Howard of Effingham, Admiral Lord Henry Seymour and Admiral Sir John Hawkins.

The memorial was unveiled on the 21st October, 1890 by Prince Alfred, the Duke of Edinburgh, on the anniversary of the Battle of Trafalgar.

The Royal Marine Memorial stands on the sea facing side of the Royal Citadel. On a pedestal stands a bronze statue of St George, measuring 7 feet 6 inches. Below the statue is a bronze plaque bearing the words:
'So he passed over and all the trumpets sounded for him on the other side'.
These words are taken from Pilgrim's Progress.
Either side of the pedestal are statues of two Royal Marines sculpted by WC Storr-Barber whose idea it was to build the monument.
The memorial was unveiled on 8th November,1921 by Earl Fortescue, the Lord Lieutenant of Devon.
An inscription reads:
Erected by the Plymouth Division Royal Marines (past and present) to the Memory of their comrades who fell in the Great War 1914-1919.
The dates 1939-1945 have also been added.

Other memorials on, or near to, the Hoe include **the Korean Veterans Memorial** erected by the Plymouth branch of the British Korean Veterans' Association and located in the Garden of Peace below the Belvedere, **the Polish Naval Memorial,** also located beneath the Belvedere, which was unveiled in 1950 and **the Prejoma Clock Memorial,** which was erected in 1965 in memory of Preston John Ball's parents. It is situated in the Hoe Lodge Gardens.

Seven:
The Victorians, Edwardians and the early 20th Century

The Hoe seems to have come alive during the Victorian and Edwardian period. Many buildings were erected during the late 1800s including Smeaton's Tower, the Pier, the Camera Obscura, the Bandstand, the Belvedere and the home of the Marine Biological Association.
All of these added to the overall attraction and beauty of the area and found a great interest with people during Victoria times. The Pier was a great draw as a meeting place with its regular shows, dances and river boat trips.

The Jubilee Bonfire, built to celebrate Queen Victoria's Diamond Jubilee Celebrations in 1897.

Another view of the Jubilee Bonfire on Plymouth Hoe in 1897.

Plymouth from the Hoe, 1896.

Three girls, in their best hats, taking a stroll below the slopes of the Hoe. In the background can be seen Smeaton's Tower and the Victorian watch tower.

Here, ladies with their parasols gather around the Victorian watch tower. It was originally built in 1877 to aid firms who were awaiting deliveries from mail steamers. A telescope was always near to hand. During the 1960s, it was used as a police and ambulance call centre. In later years, it just became somewhere to store deckchairs. Nowadays, it doesn't seem to be used for much at all.

A Victorian lady and her daughter standing below the South African War Memorial. Sheep can be seen grazing in the background.

Queen Victoria's Diamond Jubilee Celebrations, 1897.

Queues form at West Hoe for a boat trip along the river.

The Belvedere on a Bank Holiday during 1897.

Two sisters posing for the camera while sheep graze nearby.

Sheep grazing on the Hoe near to the Boer War Memorial. It's hard to imagine that farmers once kept their sheep on the Hoe but they were once a common sight there. In the early 19th century, the area was known as 'Hoe Fields' and cows also grazed there. They would certainly have kept the grass short!

A photo showing crowds gathering around the popular Camera Obscura. The Hoe constable can be seen in his top hat and uniform keeping order. The Obscura stood above the Belvedere and is now long gone. Some people think that the Obscura building is the one that remains in front of Smeaton's Tower but this is not the case. The Obscura had a small camera on top and it was possible to view a full colour, moving image of Plymouth Sound on a white screen inside the darkened room. It seems amazing now that people would queue and pay to see an image they could see by just standing outside but these were the days before popular photography and, anything like this, people found amazing and it would draw huge crowds. Even today though, a camera obscura seems very impressive. It was a very simple apparatus with a pin hole camera, a lens and a screen which has been suggested was a tablecloth provided by the owner. The owner can be seen in this picture by the doorway collecting entrance fees. The Obscura was built in approximately 1827 and it was destroyed by strong gales in 1840. The Obscura was rebuilt by William Sampson in 1842 and run by his wife until it was demolished in 1889 by the council who were making improvements to the Hoe.

Norrington's Fountain was unveiled in 1881. On the side is inscribed,
'Presented to the town of Plymouth by Charles Norrington in memory of
his wife, Marianne Norrington,1881. Thirsty and ye gave me drink'.
The fountain was originally on the site of the bowling green near Osborne
Terrace. Charles Norrington was Mayor of Plymouth in both 1864 and
1881.

The Queen Victoria Jubilee fountain, above, is now long gone but once stood in front of the Belvedere where the Bullring had stood earlier in the 19th century. The fountain was donated by James King who was then the mayor of Plymouth.

The Belvedere was erected in 1891.The pillars in the upper tiers came from a previous market building. The Bullring was so called because during the 1600s, bulls were tethered here and baited by bulldogs for sport and apparently to make the bull's flesh more tender. Amazingly, butchers were fined if they didn't carry out baiting. The practice was banned in 1815.

The last political meeting in the Bullring was in June 1882.However,in 1891,a byelaw was passed banning public meetings altogether on the Hoe.

An early shot of the Cage Walk.

This picture shows the walkway, known as Cage Walk, between the Hoe and the Barbican at Lambhay Point. At one time, the Hoe was separated from the Barbican by a tunnel with a wire grill. The Hoe finished at the western end of the Citadel. In the Winter evenings, cooks at the Elphinstone Barracks would sometimes hand dough buns through the gates to waiting children. Before the war, it was demolished so that the road from the Hoe could carry on right down to the Barbican.

The view looking towards West Hoe.

An early bowling match with Smeaton's Tower in the background. Most men are in suits though some have taken their jackets off and rolled up their sleeves to play. One man, on the left of the picture, is wearing a straw boater.

A 1920s shot of Plymouth Hoe. Smeaton's Tower is painted as it is today.

Two ladies and a man sit close to Drake's statue. In the background, can be seen the Armada Memorial and the statue of Britannia which celebrate the English victory over the Spanish Armada.

Elliot Terrace, in the middle of this picture with the chimneys, was a very fashionable place to live in its day and was the home to Lord and Lady Astor.

An aerial shot of the Hoe featuring the bandstand and the pier. Smeaton's Tower and the Naval War Memorial can be seen in the background.

A view looking out towards the Pier and Plymouth Sound. The man on the left has a pair of binoculars probably watching the people and the boats.

A pre-war view of the Hoe probably taken in the later 1930s.It looks much the same as it does today apart from the bandstand still being in place.

Eight:
The People

Members of the Plymouth Hoe Boat Club in 1925.

Three sailors take it easy on the Hoe.

People gathering around the popular bandstand near to Smeaton's Tower.

A band surround a man in a straw boater who is entertaining the gathered spectators.

Nancy Astor's receiving a package from her postman who delivered her election mail in 1923.

Lady Astor was born in Danville in Virginia on 19th May 1879. Her father, Chiswell Dabney Langhorne was a successful railway developer, a profession which made him very wealthy. In 1897, the then Nancy Langhorne married Robert Gould Shaw but they divorced in 1903 and she moved to England where she met the wealthy American, Waldorf Astor. They married in 1906. Waldorf was the Conservative MP for the Sutton Ward of Plymouth. They made their home at Cliveden in Bristol but later moved to Plymouth.

Nancy did a lot of work to help the poor and underprivileged of Plymouth and she was much respected for this. In 1912, she opened day nurseries for the children of poor mothers who needed to work to feed and clothe their families.

When Waldorf became 2nd Viscount Astor, when his father died in 1919, his seat became available and Nancy put herself forward as a candidate. On 1st December 1919, she became the first woman to hold a seat in the House of Commons.

Both Lord and Lady Astor became well loved by Plymouthians and when Waldorf became Lord Mayor in 1939, Nancy became his Mayoress. She did much work during the war years to support the victims and homeless of the German bombings and she greatly increased the moral of the people of Plymouth during their hardships. Famously, she introduced dancing on the Hoe during the war years.
She died on the 2nd May, 1964.

Crowds gather to see Lady Astor on the Hoe.

Queen Marie of Rumania (now Romania) visiting Plymouth Hoe on 31st May 1924. She was the granddaughter of Queen Victoria.

Men playing bowls in the shadow of the Naval War Memorial. Bowls has always been a very popular sport on the Hoe.

A photo taken just before the Second World War. This photo was taken in the Hoe Lodge Gardens. Two ladies admire the flowers. The bandstand is still in place and Smeaton's Tower stands beside the Victorian Watch Tower in the background.

Nine:
Snow on the Hoe

The Hoe has seen many downfalls of snow over the years and it has always provided great entertainment especially for children who have enjoyed building snowmen, having snowball fights and sledging.

Sheep beside the path on the way towards the Hoe.

Victorian children enjoying a snowball fight. One has cleverly hidden behind the snowman while the picture is taken to make it appear that the snowman is joining in.

The slopes of the Hoe covered in snow. The Jubilee fountain was still in place, at the time, situated within the Bullring.

A Victorian lady making her way up the Hoe slopes. The Pier and the Belvedere can be seen in the picture. The tram lines are the only clear area on the road while the surrounding area is thick with snow.

A later snow scene in front of Drake's statue. A boy on the left is being pulled along on a sledge by his dad while three other people have a snowball fight.

Ten:
The Pier

Work began on Plymouth's Pier in 1880. It was the idea of Mr Edward
Lancaster of Old Town Street who had put the proposal forward in 1878.
Workman's huts were erected in the area of the Bullring and in August
1880, the Marine Piers Company invited members of the public to invest
in shares in the building. It was announced that the Pier would measure
610 feet long and 60 feet wide. It was suggested that a pavilion at the end
of the pier would be built which could hold 2,500 people. Objections were
raised though because it was felt that this would block out people's view
of Drake's Island. The plan was quickly abandoned. It was hoped that the
Pier would be opened by the Summer of 1881 but amazingly only 20 men
were employed on site by the original contractor, Laidlaw Sons and Caine
of Glasgow. The Western Daily Mercury reported at the end of 1880, that
the chances of a quick completion were slim.

In 1882, after financial problems, a new contractor was employed, a Mr C
Daniel of London, who was a member of the Royal Yacht Club. When he
took over, only the first section of iron work of the pier had been
constructed. He quickly employed many local carpenters to lay the pine
flooring.

The total cost of the construction was £45,000. Of this, £17,000 had been
spent locally on labour and materials.

A photo of the entrance to the Pier. A horse drawn tram waits outside with an advertisement for Spooners and Co on its side. From the clock, it is 12.30pm. The sign below the clock reads, 'Concerts every afternoon and evening'. There are metal turnstyle gates at the admission points at the entrance to the pier. Various posters advertise the pier's attractions.

The Pier was officially opened on 29th May 1884. Guests included the Mayor, John Greenway, who was presented with a silver gilt key to unlock the main gate. Thirty thousand people turned up for the ceremony of which ten thousand were said to have been on the Pier itself. The Band of the Royal Marines played while Baron Grant, the chairman of the directors, and the contractor, Mr C Daniel, welcomed guests. The local paper reported that, 'Nellie, the Plymouth flower girl, was as enterprising as usual, having brought some handsome bouquets and button-holes'.

The Pier consisted of 140 columns embedded in solid rock. It measured a total of 420 feet. Inside the banjo area of the Pier, there was a stationers, a bookstall, a post office, a reading room and very popular slot machines. Facing seawards, there were refreshment rooms ran by Mr H Matthews. Two iron staircases led down to the waters edge so that people could board pleasure steamers that took them on trips around the Sound and up the River Tamar and Yealm.

The Concert Pavilion which was to seat 2,000 people wasn't completed until 1891.

In the early days, the Pier had its problems. Amazingly, it was sold to a fish merchant, a Mr Walter Kay of Citadel Road, in 1887.The Pier had been put up for auction at The Mart at Tokenhouse Yard, London. It was

Pier Pavilion & Cafe

General Manager - - JACK MERRETT.

Concert Party Performances

3-15 p.m.   Twice daily   7-45 p.m.

(From June 3rd onwards)

THE RIVIERA REVELS

The Super Road Show produced by Harry Benet.

NOTE REDUCED PRICES:

1/= and 6d. (including Pier Toll and Tax)

DANCING

Every Wednesday, 10 p.m. to 1 a.m. and
Saturday, 10 p.m. to 11-45 p.m.

CONCERTS EVERY SUNDAY

3-15 p.m. and 8 p.m.

CAFE OPEN DAILY

Rowing Boats on Hire AT WEST HOE PIER

For Special Attractions see Daily Papers

An advert for the Pier announcing the arrival of Harry Benet's, 'Riviera Revels'.

sold, after much bidding, for a total of £12,000.The pier only reached this grand total because the auctioneer, Sir John Whitaker Ellis MP, suggested that the Plymouth Corporation would wake up to the value of the Pier and it could well be sold on for a profit. This encouraged people to bid though it appears that there wasn't as much interest in the Pier as would have been expected.

In March, 1888, the Western Morning News reported that, at last, the Pier was getting something it was long over due - a lick of paint! The vanes were re-tipped with gilt and new paint and varnish was applied wherever possible. Two kiosks at the entrance were let out to James Denham and Cuthbert Collingwood who were tobacconists and Georgina Tierney who sold fancy goods. There was also a call office installed by the United Telephone Company. After a complete overhaul, admission was announced as 1d. Books of concession tickets could also be bought.

The Plymouth Ladies' Swimming Club and the Seven O'Clock Regulars used the Pier as their headquarters and they gave swimming and diving demonstrations each year in July during the Plymouth Regatta.

In the Winter months, the Pier featured mainly concerts but in the Summer there were allsorts of activities going on including wrestling, dancing, boxing and the ever popular roller skating. Military bands would also play on Sunday evenings.

The Pier acquired its steamboats in 1910 for trips up and down the river but by 1922, interest in the Pier was waning and the company disposed of some of its steamers.

A motor show was held in the Pavilion in 1932 which showed off the new Ford 8 horse powered car.

Towards the end of its life, the Pier had seen better days and by 1934, a loss was recorded of £1,276. However, the accounts of 1935 showed a brighter picture and the Pier was valued at £69,000. However, a plan to sell the Pier failed and in 1938,the Receiver was called in. The concern of what to do with the Pier was solved three years later by the Luftwaffe when they bombed Plymouth and the Pier was completely destroyed. There was no doubt that the Pier had had its problems and had lost money but it was fondly remembered and sadly missed by many people at the time. In 1953, the remnants of the Pier were removed by the Eglinton Brothers at a cost of £4,754. It's possible to see today where the entrance to the Pier once stood opposite to the Belvedere, the path bends in slightly and a row of seats have been put in its place. It would be great to see it rebuilt one day but perhaps the era of the Pier is, unfortunately, now long dead.

Regatta Day by the Pier. Crowds gather around the Pier to watch the various events taking place in the Sound. There are many posh hats worn by the female spectators. By the clock on the Pier, the time appears to be 4.55pm.

An early shot of the Pier. There are hand carts and their operators waiting on the roadside. It's 1.15 pm and a large sign under the clock reads,' Lieut Charles Godfrey and his Band'. Hoardings at the entrance advertise Beards and Co the Jewellers, The Daily Mercury and Beechams Pills. A sign to the right reads, 'Excursion Steamers from this Pier. Tolls Free, For Yealm'.

The pier at 4 o'clock in 1925. A sign on the Pavilion reads,' Concerts, Cafe, Steamers' and there's a hoarding advertising, 'The Independent'. The lady sat on the wall sums up the fashion of the day.

PIER PAVILION & CAFE

General Manager—J. MERRETT.

THE HOME OF

CONCERTS
CABARETS
CARNIVALS

Winter Dances every Saturday.
Summer Dances every Wednesday & Friday.

"THE PIER"—THE CENTRE OF ALL ATTRACTIONS.

TELEPHONE NO. 941.

An advert for the Pier - 'The centre for all attractions'.

A view of the Pier looking back towards the Belvedere. A sign to the left reads, 'S Fox Oil' and in the distance, at the beginning of the Pier, there is a sign advertising, 'Beecham's Pills'.

The Concert Pavilion at the end of the Pier. Friday nights featured the popular sport, all-in wrestling.

Small boats sail near to the Pier.

A pleasure boat, fully laden, prepares to leave for a trip up the river.

A man dives from the Pier above an advert for cocoa.

Amazingly, this photo was taken in 1896. Above, is a sign advertising, 'Spooner and Co'. It's interesting to see the swimsuits of the day. Looking at a photo like this, it makes you wonder what sort of lives they all led. Unfortunately, their names aren't known.

Another photo taken in 1896 and this one features one of the young men in the previous group photo. This appears to have been taken below the Pier and it looks like he might have just been in for a dip.

Two side views of the Pier. In the background of the top picture are two Training Brigs. The ships were used for the training of young seamen.

Eleven:
The Fair

The fair has been a popular attraction on the Hoe since the early 1900s and the tradition has continued until today. Perhaps one of the most well known fairground companies in the area was Whiteleggs. Thomas Whitelegg and Sons were based in Plymouth and were founded in 1920. The went on to be well known all over the west of England. After the Second Word War, the firm was run by Thomas's three sons, Tommy, Bibsey and Arthur. Whitleggs became the largest fairground operator in the region and dominated the fairground scene during the 1950s and 1960s with their huge selection of rides and amusements.

This photo shows Hancock's Circus at West Hoe. Attractions included the 'Joy Wheel' , the Carousel, 'Hancock's Motorcycles' and the 'Cave' where children baked potatoes. The Helter Skelter was another very popular attraction.

Whiteleggs fair on the Hoe Promenade. The Naval War Memorial is on the left. There are many popular attractions shown including the Helter Skelter and Big Top Speedway.

In the foreground is the rifle range wall and in the background is the Pier. Attractions here include the Helter Skelter and the Carousel ride.

People gather around to have a go at this attraction. The smiling owner holds several balls and it appears that these are to be used to throw at the metal faces in the background. To the right of the attraction's owner, is a large selection of Charlie Chaplin type walking sticks and it appears that these might be the prizes.

The Gondola Boats at West Hoe were a popular attraction. One man on the end gondola is swinging standing up and it appears as if he is just about to go over the top. The Carousel and Helter Skelter rides can be seen in the background.

A close up of the exciting Helter Skelter ride.

The Carousel ride which has mainly adults as its customers. Foreign visitors were amazed that our carousels turned clockwise as theirs turned anti-clockwise.

A man and young lady sell balls to throw at the Coconut Shy. The prizes would include any coconuts dislodged. Sometimes there would be other prizes to be won too.

The Motor Switchback was a popular ride for everyone and charged 1d for children and 2d for adults. In the days when there were few cars, this was as close as many people got to driving.

The Rifle Range. An attraction for all young men who fancied themselves as sharp shooters and who wanted to impress their girlfriends.

Twelve:
On the Waterfront

Swimming and waterside events have always proved to be very popular attractions on the Hoe. Annual regattas and competitions between local swimming clubs were always a big draw, with crowds of spectators attending.

Most of the swimming events in these photos seem to just involve men, though there were also ladies rowing teams which took part regularly in various regattas.

In this pictures, several men practice their life saving skills. People watch on from a boat behind and several men, perhaps judges, are wearing boaters. The swimming costumes have certainly changed over the years!

Judges watch on as competitors take part in a swimming race.

This photo shows the 'Seven o'clock Regulars' who were guests of the 'Tinside Champs'. They all have their own various names related to nuts on their tops. These include, 'Grape Nuts', 'What a Nut', 'A Funny Nut', 'Mr Chestnut', 'Miss Walnut', 'Mr Beech', 'Mr Almond' and 'Mr Coconut' etc. Their leader is called, 'The Kernel'.

Boys practising for their lifesaving drill. Many men wearing boaters, sit on the boat behind and the man directing the events has a loud hailer.

This photo shows Alderman Henry Hurrell with the Seven o'clock Regulars. As shown in a previous photo, they donned pyjamas and sugar loaf hats during gala events while the 'Shaggey Pool Stragglers' dressed as the Mayor and other members of the Corporation. The Seven o'clock Regulars Swimming Club was founded in 1911.

Here, a large crowd has gathered for the Plymouth Diving Association's competitions during Civic Week in July 1933. The festivities ended with a huge firework display on the 22nd July which was watched by 50,000 spectators.

This photo shows the children's pool known by various names over the years including Shaggey Pool and Piskies Pool.

A view of the Hoe from the Sound with Smeaton's Tower sitting prominent on top. It's hard to see in this picture but there are thousands of people watching the events below and a few rowing boats can be seen taking part in the Regatta.

This photo shows the Men's Pool which was opened in 1907. All day swimming was allowed in 1860 but the local newspaper reported that dead cats and sewerage often spoiled it! There was also a ladies pool which was opened in 1877, west of Tinside. In 1919, mixed bathing was allowed.

A sailor watches a yacht in the Sound as ladies, gents and their children enjoy the attraction of being beside the water.

Children playing in the water near to West Hoe. The sign reads, 'West Hoe Pier. All excursion steamers leave this pier. Tolls free'.

Two small boys paddling in the Sound with West Hoe behind them.

Children playing on the steps leading into the water. Here, the railings disappear into the high tide.

Children enjoying swimming in the Sound while others gather around the diving board.

A family gather on rocks near to The Sound.

A boat sails slowly past the Hoe. The number on the side is 'PH 229'.

Thirteen:
The Lido

The Lido was designed by S Wibberley, a City Engineer, who also designed the surrounding buildings built into the cliffside. It featured a classic semi-circle pool with three fountains cascading water into the pool. The water was drawn from the sea and pumped through the cascades to give a complete change of water every four hours.

The Lido was officially opened on 2nd October 1935 by The Lord Mayor, Lieutenant-Commander EW Rogers. The three fountains were floodlit at night and gave three different colour changes.

Art Deco in style, in it's heyday, it would have been a glorious site. It was described in 1935 as 'one of the finest open-sea bathing centres in the country'. Orchestras played above in the terraces as people swam.

It was also once a popular venue for beauty contests. One of the things that made the Lido so popular was the interest then in the new continental activity, sunbathing. This must have seemed very modern at a time when people still went to the beach dressed in their Sunday best and many men's idea of sunbathing would be to take off their thick jacket, roll their sleeves up and put a knotted hanky on their heads! There certainly wouldn't be a bikini in sight!

During the war years, people used the Lido to wash in after spending hours clearing up the bomb ravaged streets of Plymouth. Unfortunately, the distinctive shape of the pool helped German bombers get their bearings as they flew towards the city during many of their raids.

Cheap holidays abroad, in later years, were blamed for the decline and

79

lack of interest in the pool. Perhaps much of the blame lay for years with the City Council and its lack of interest in the Hoe and its foreshore. Even with cheap holidays abroad, the foreshore was very popular throughout this time, it was just allowed to get more run down year by year.
The Lido fell into disrepair in the 1980s and it was closed in 1992.It seems a shame that the Hoe foreshore was ever allowed to get in such a poor state. It was only a vigorous campaign by local people that saved it from being lost forever. However, it has now been restored at a cost of £3.4 million and it makes a great feature on the Hoe though, perhaps, it has lost the attraction that it once had. Work on the foreshore still continues and hopefully, one day, the area will be restored to its full glory.
The Lido and changing rooms are now Grade II listed.

The busy Lido showing all three fountains. People can be seen sitting on deckchairs around the edges of the pool watching the happy swimmers.

Fourteen:
During the Second World War

The face of Plymouth changed forever during the Second World War. Many of its buildings were obliterated. Although not unscathed, much of Plymouth Hoe didn't fare as bad as the city centre though several landmarks such as the Pier and the bandstand were destroyed forever.

A picture of Drake's statue with a barrage balloon floating behind.

Digging for Victory on the Hoe. 'Digging for Victory' was a slogan used during war time to encourage people to grow vegetables in any available spot to ensure that we had plenty of food supplies. Here, men, possibly of the Home Guard, dig a patch of the Hoe so that potatoes can be planted.

Ambulances parked on the Hoe marked, 'Bundles for Britain' .These were generously donated to Plymouth by the Americans. These were given by the Cincinnati Branch.

This is a photo of the remains of the bandstand after a bombing raid. Anything that could be saved for scrap was rescued. Here, a barrage balloon team salvage anything they can for the war effort. Unfortunately, the bandstand was never rebuilt.

Bomb damage on the Hoe Slopes. On the night of the 5th July 1941, the Hoe area came under attack. On the same night, bombs were also dropped on Hartley, Crownhill, Keyham, Laira, Devonport and Beacon Park. Near to the Hoe, the Windsor Arms and nearby houses received direct hits resulting in two families being completely wiped out.

This photo shows all that remained of the Pier's entrance after it was bombed. It's hard to imagine the once grand frontage of this popular attraction from the debris shown in this picture.

The Pier in a sorry state after being destroyed by enemy bombing in 1941. The Pier remained until 1952 when the council decided to remove its rusting remains.

Dancing on the Hoe brought many people together during the war years.

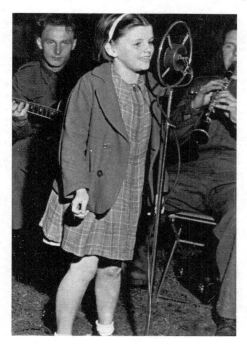

A young girl singing at an open air concert on the Hoe. She is accompanied by a military band. Dancing on the Hoe continued for many years and a huge dance was held to celebrate VE Day on the 8th May 1945.

American personnel dancing on the hoe near to Smeaton's Tower.
This photo was probably taken in 1943, or soon after, when there was a
huge American presence in the city.

An American soldier dances with Lady Astor near to Drake's statue.
Al fresco dancing on the Hoe began during the first week of May 1941 and
was a success from the beginning. The idea was first suggested by the
Lord Mayor, Lord Astor. Lady Astor regularly took part and among her
dancing partners was the Duke of Kent.

Two photos showing dancing on the Hoe. These pictures show many
sailors and military service men dancing with local girls.

Lady Astor dancing with a sailor. Noel Coward, who was a friend of the Astors, said at the time, 'After all that devastation, on a Summer evening, people were dancing on the Hoe. It made me cry - the bravery, the gallantry, the Englishness of it!'

This photo shows the Terrace at Leigham Street which was badly bombed during the war. The houses were situated above the old quarry at West Hoe, near to Cliff Road. They had excellent views across the Sound towards Mount Edgcumbe and Jennycliff. After the war, the site was cleared and the Quality Hotel (formerly the Forte Posthouse) now stands on the site.

A ceremony in front of the Lord Mayor attended by the city's police force.

Fifteen:
After the War

After the war, the Hoe was still seen as a place of entertainment. The huge stretch of the promenade and Smeaton's Tower still looked glorious on a sunny day. Evening dancing continued and famous bands as well as Naval, Military and Air Force bands were engaged to play on the Hoe during the Summer season.

Smeaton's Tower was open to the public and there was a charge of 2d to climb the narrow staircase to the top. Other attractions included the Lido and the Hoe foreshore where beach huts could be hired for two shillings a day during Spring and five shillings a day during the Summer.

Deckchairs proved very popular and were to be found on all parts of the Hoe including the foreshore. The charge was 3d or a weekly ticket could be bought for two shillings.

During the 1950s, visitors were admitted to the Marine Biological Laboratory and Aquarium for 6d. The Citadel also welcomed visitors and the ramparts were open to the public from 2pm to 6pm on Wednesdays, Saturdays and Sundays.

There was always plenty to do. Including bathing, there was also the attraction of going on a excursion steamer, going boating or playing tennis, bowling or putting.

The Lido charged 6d for adults and 4d for children. The admission also covered the charge of the use of a deckchair. There was also the opportunity to be taught by a swimming instructor for the charge of one shilling a lesson.

Ladies bowling on the Hoe, 1950.

Bowling has always proved a popular pastime for both men and women on the Hoe. During the 1950s, the charge was one shilling an hour to play on the Hoe and 9d an hour in various other parks around the city. The Sir Francis Drake Bowling Club was founded in 1907. The cost for developing the site was £65 and is the same area used today, however, the Francis Drake Bowling Club severed its association with the Hoe Bowling green in 1922 and opened their own green and pavilion at Whiteford Road in Mannamead in that year.

Men taking part in a bowling match. Most are wearing cloth caps and have their shirt sleeves rolled up.

The Hoe Cafe.

An old pavilion serving tea stood on this spot until it was bombed in the Second World War. In 1947, it was decided to build a temporary structure as a new cafe. A 'Blister' hangar was agreed to be the most practical building available at the time and the council acquired one from the air ministry for a cost of £100. To convert the hangar into a cafe, walls had to be partitioned off and flooring was laid using reclaimed timber. With drainage, lighting and equipment etc the total construction bill came to £4000. The cafe also included a platform with a musicians gallery. Before the war, all the major cafes in the city boasted their own musical entertainment.

The cafe was opened on 16th July 1947 by the Lord Mayor, Mr W H Taylor. The takings in the first ten days were £700. The funny thing was, that also in this ten day period, other things were taken too, including fifty glasses, twenty four tea spoons, thirty plates, twenty forks and twenty five knives! Maybe the war had left people short of household utensils!

The cafe served the people visiting the Hoe well and it didn't close until 1981.It was demolished in 1982.

Devonshire PLYMOUTH

GRAND HOTEL THE HOE

DIRECTLY FACING THE SEA · FULLY LICENSED

NEW
COCKTAIL LOUNGE

Terms from 17/6 Room and Breakfast

27/6 inclusive per Day for Minimum of 3-day Stay

Telephone : 4393

100 Bedrooms, all with running Hot & Cold Water. Private Suites. Lift. Electric Fires for Bedrooms. Lounges with open fires. Sun Terrace Enclosed. Lock-up Garages. R.A.C. and A.A. Gentlemen's Hairdressing Saloon. Open All the Year Round. Tariff and Further Details from P. G. H. Langford, Manager . .

Proprietors : HEATHS (PLYMOUTH) LTD.

An advert for the Grand Hotel, 1950.

Laurel and Hardy stayed at the Grand Hotel during the 1950s. They were due to start a series of shows at the Palace Theatre on 17th May 1954 in a production called, 'Birds of a Feather'. Oliver Hardy suffered from a bad bout of flu and had a mild heart attack so the show was cancelled. Ollie rested at the Grand Hotel for the rest of his stay and Stan later sent the manager of the Palace Theatre an apology letter.

The hotel has seen many famous guests over the years including Noel Coward, Edward Heath and Lord and Lady Astor who, over breakfast at the hotel, decided that Plymouth was the place where they wished to live.

Sixteen:
The Hoe in the 1960s

The Hoe continued to be very popular throughout the 1960s. One new addition was the building of the Hoe Theatre. During 1969, the Easter attractions at the theatre included a season of plays while the Summer attraction was Billie and Trevor George's 'Happy People and Lucky Stars', which ran nightly at 7.30pm.The admission was six shillings. On Sunday of the same year, the entertainment was provided by Reg Robins and his Kortne Hungarian Orchestra and the admission was three shillings. There was also a Christmas Pantomime which opened on Boxing Day.

The Hoe saw a visit from the Beatles in September 1967 when they were filming, 'The Magical Mystery Tour'. Clips shown on local tv showed the Beatles walking up to the Hoe near to the Naval War Memorial and sitting on the banks of the Hoe slopes looking out towards the Sound.

A beauty contest held by the Lido pool. It's interesting to see the hair styles and clothing of the day. The winner is wearing a Miss Plymouth sash which is dated 1967.She also has a cup and an envelope. This is the sort of event that it seems very unlikely would ever take place by the Lido again.

The very popular Hoe Theatre. Known as 'The Hoe Summer Theatre', it was built in 1962 and replaced a marquee which had stood in the same spot previously. The former marquee was also known as the 'Hoe Theatre' and was erected in 1950.

The Hoe Summer Theatre stayed open for twenty years and finally closed in May 1982, which was the year that the Theatre Royal opened in the City Centre. Demolition started on 18th May and took about six weeks. Interestingly, during this process, one of Robert Lenkiewicz's murals was discovered inside. It had been wallpapered over but builders managed to save part of it. It had originally been painted by Robert Lenkiewicz in 1970. The mural was unfinished and perhaps this was because of comments from a Mr Brian Rabin, from a meeting of the Plymouth Junior Chamber Of Commerce in 1976, who said at the time, ' It appals me that our civic leaders can frequent the Hoe Theatre without throwing up their hands in horror. The mural on the wall of the foyer shows people putting out their tongues and using Churchillian gestures. We should try to get it whitewashed and restored to order. It's our theatre and this is just an obscene gesture to the people of Plymouth. And when will it be finished? We should invite vandals to come and scrawl on it.'

Finally, in 1978, the council decided to wall paper over Lenkiewicz's mural. It had taken four months to paint and measured approximately 60 feet.

Lenkiewicz congratulated the city entertainments officer for 'his remarkable good taste' when the mural was removed. The mural had originally been painted free of charge because of the Hoe Theatre's lack of funds.

The Hoe Theatre with the Civic Centre in the background.

Interestingly, the land where the theatre stood was also the site of public hangings several hundreds of years before. It's still possible to work out where the theatre once stood as the grass grows a different colour in this patch.

The 1969 Plymouth Guide described the Hoe within its pages. It said:

Beyond the foreshore extend the sparkling waters of the Sound, the ocean gateway to England, and the starting point for centuries of many a famous sea voyage, including the most recent of all, that of Sir Francis Chichester.

With the opportunity to laze in a deckchair on the broad promenade and gaze upon the scene, enlivened by the colour and movement from the thronging crowds on the coastal road below, and the sight of gaily coloured yachts skimming over the water, the holiday maker has to reconcile a desire to spend his days on the Hoe with a no less insistent desire to explore the City.

Also, during the 1960s, the Gus Honeybun trains appeared at West Hoe. These were very popular with young children who loved seeing Gus Honeybun on Westward Television and enjoyed getting their birthday requests read out by local presenters on the tv, aided by Gus doing many tricks including head stands and bunny hops. The trains are still there but Gus is long forgotten. Replacement rabbits (not Gus Honeybun) feature but perhaps today's children and their parents wonder why a rabbit is stuffed down the funnel of a train!

The Fair with the Big Wheel in the background.

This photo shows the ever popular fair on the Hoe. It looks like the Lord Mayor and his wife have just been on the dodgems, complete with chauffeur!

A family plays golf at the putting green.

The putting green was always a popular family attraction during the holiday season. The course had eighteen holes and two greens. It's still there and people still putt but perhaps it isn't as popular as it once was. Another attraction, mentioned in the 1969 Plymouth Guide, was the 'Holiday Bowls Competition'. The entry fee was 2 shillings and 6d and the contest was held every Thursday between 10th July and 28th August,1969. If you were lucky enough to win, the prize included a trophy and £51 in vouchers! It would have been a lot of money 40 years ago.
All the pools on the Hoe were used at the time and at most times, during the Summer, were very busy as were the diving boards.
Probably the most popular activity on the Hoe though was 'people watching', either from the Hoe Slopes or from the many deckchairs spread around. Ice cream vans lined Madeira Road and huge queues formed at each of them. Cafes were also packed out especially the main 'hangar type' Hoe Cafe leading up towards the Hoe.
During the Summer of 1968, the chimps from the PG Tips adverts visited the Hoe. The adverts were very popular at the time with schoolchildren everywhere repeating the catchphrases, 'Can you ride tandem?' and 'Coo-ee! Mr Shifter!'. There was a large turn out but some of the crowd weren't too happy when the chimps appeared.
'But where are the talking ones?' someone said. They obviously felt that if they wanted to see ordinary non-talking chimps, they could have gone to Plymouth Zoo! Television was relatively new at the time and many people believed just what they saw on the screen!

Hedley Claxton presented Gaytime at the Hoe Theatre in the 1960s.
I somehow think it would attract a whole different audience nowadays!

Two more adverts for the Hoe Theatre. The top advert advertises 'Starlight Rendezvous' featuring Len Howe and Audrey Maye. The advert below advertises 'Gaytime', which it says is 'a beautifully dressed and staged Summer musical.

Sunbathing on the Hoe. There was a time when deckchairs were to be found all over the Hoe. You would find one you liked and sooner or later an attendant would come around and charge you for the privilege and give you a ticket to say that you'd paid. The deckchairs disappeared for years and then recently made a reappearance. I wonder where they had been for all those years?

Deckchairs along Madeira Road overlooking the Sound.
'Bring your knitting, Elsie!'

A family eat overlooking Tinside pool. The Hoe seemed a lot busier place during the 1960s and 1970s. It still gets lots of visitors but not on the scale that it once did.

ALL THE NICE GIRLS...

LOVE A

Wall's
ICE CREAM

A 1960s advert for Wall's Ice Cream popular with many Hoe visitors. This has been aimed at the Plymouth market and features a returning sailor.

Seventeen:
The Hoe in the 1970s

The swimming pools around the Hoe, particularly the Lido, proved very popular during the 1970s. Regular events took place on the promenade on the Hoe in the 1970s. As well as the fair, there were also jousting events and even a visit by apes from the popular tv series of the time, 'Planet of the Apes'. Other attractions included the Red Arrows, the Air Show, the many sailing events and the Radio One Road Show with disc jockeys of the day including Emperor Rosko who visited in 1975.

The big event on the Hoe, during the 1970s, was the visit by the Queen and the Duke of Edinburgh in 1977 as part of the Silver Jubilee celebrations. Thousands lined the streets of Plymouth and huge crowds gathered as she arrived on the Hoe.

One of the hottest ever Summers was in 1976 and the Hoe was packed with sunbathers enjoying the endless weeks of sunshine.

A photo showing people relaxing on one of the sun terraces. At one time, deckchairs were a very common site on the Hoe in the Summer and made their owners a good living. It looks like some of the people above have brought their own here though!

A 1970s photo showing Smeaton's Tower when it was painted white. The fashions have changed but little else.

Two boys looking out over the sunbathers towards the Sound.

It's easier to keep 'em happy with Lyons Maid ice cream

An advert in the Plymouth Guide for Lyons Maid Ice Cream which needed endless supplies to cope with the demand on Plymouth Hoe.

Eighteen:
Plymouth Hoe Today

Take a walk around Plymouth Hoe today and many of the attractions and buildings mentioned in this book are still to be found. Smeaton's Tower takes pride of place and is an instant recognised landmark. Nearby, proudly stands Drake's Statue, The Naval War Memorial and the Armada Memorial. Many of the other memorials mentioned in this book are to be found nearby. Strolling along the promenade, towards West Hoe, the Belvedere appears on your left whilst, to your right, can be seen Elliot Terrace, once the home of Lord and Lady Astor. Nearby is the building that was once the Grand Hotel.

The Hoe has seen changes though. The Camera Obscura has now gone as have the bandstand and the Pier. The Plymouth Dome has appeared on the slopes but has never proved as popular as the cafe that once stood there. Also gone are the Hoe Cafe and the Hoe Theatre. The Grand now stands empty after it was devastated by fire in 2003.The Lido after many years of disrepair is now once again open but much of the foreshore has seen better days.

All in all, the attraction and appeal of the Hoe still remains and it gives great pleasure to local people as well as drawing many visitors from the rest of the UK and from all over the world. It's one of those places that is instantly recognisable from photos and, hopefully, it's appeal will never fade.

A view of the Hoe from the Sound. Smeaton's Tower stands prominent in the middle of the picture with the Naval Memorial to the right. On the left can be seen Madeira Road and in the foreground is the Lido.

Smeaton's Tower now painted in its original heritage colours.

Silhouettes of the RAF and Allied Forces Monument, Smeaton's Tower
and the Armada Memorial.

Smeaton's Tower and Drake's statue on an Autumn day.

Drake's Statue still proudly surveys the Sound.

Two views of the Naval War Memorial.

Once the Hoe Lodge, now the Valentis Cafe Bar.

A silver bird now stands in the Hoe Lodge gardens.

The Prejoma Clock standing in what was once the Hoe Lodge Gardens.
Twice a day, it tells the right time!

The Hoe Slopes. Apart from the cars, little seems to have changed since Victorian days.

Looking towards Smeaton's Tower from the Belvedere.

Two photos of the refurbished Tinside Lido, now once again attracting visitors.

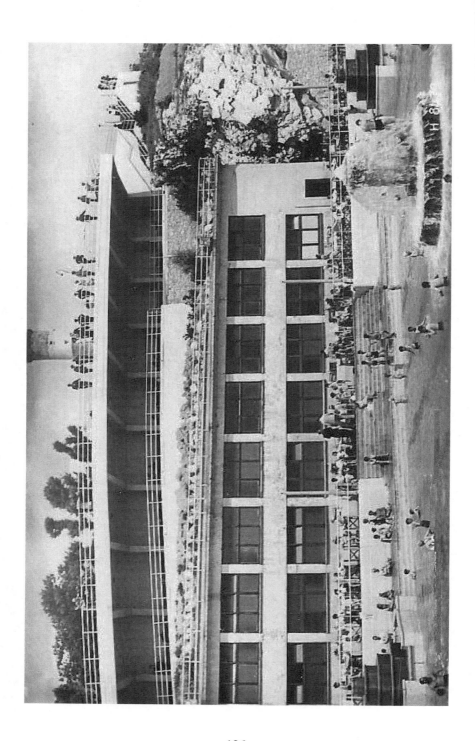

126

By the same author :

St Budeaux

St Budeaux
A history of St Budeaux, Plymouth. Contains over 150 old photos and illustrations.
108 pages.
Price : £9.99.
ISBN-13: 978-0955427763.

Saltash
Passage

Saltash Passage
A history of Saltash Passage, Plymouth. Contains over 140 old photos and illustrations.
104 pages.
Price : £9.99.
ISBN-13: 978-0955427732.

Sampans, Banyans and Rambutans
A Childhood in Singapore and Malaya
A childhood spent in Singapore and Malaya in the 1960s as part of a Naval family.
104 pages.
Price : £7.99.
ISBN-13: 978-0955427701.

Memories of Singapore and Malaya

Memories of Singapore and Malaya during the 1950s,1960s and 1970s through the eyes of servicemen and their families.
Contains 230 photos.
194 pages.
Price : £9.99.
ISBN-13: 978-0955427756.